SEE

& OTHER POEMS

Also by Jerome Rothenberg

JEROME ROTHENBERG

SEEDINGS

& OTHER POEMS

A NEW DIRECTIONS BOOK

1808-1

Some of these poems have appeared previously in *Improvisations* (Dieu Donné Press, New York, 1991), *An Oracle for Delfi* (Membrane Press, Milwaukee, 1995), and *Pictures of the Crucifixion* (Granary Books, New York, 1996), all by Jerome Rothenberg; in a broadside (*A Message for the One Who Walks Here, Yes*) from Woodland Pattern (Milwaukee, 1994); and in the following magazines and anthologies: *10 Ans de poésie directe* (Centre International de Poésie Marseille, 1995), *Action Poétique* (Paris), *Antologija americke poezije* (Novi Sad, Yugoslavia), *Apex of the M*, βητα [Vita] (Athens), *Camera Obscura* (Athens), *Exquisite Corpse, Exploded Views: A San Diego Spoken Word Compilation* (CD anthology, 1995), *The Gertrude Stein Awards in Innovative American Poetry* (Sun & Moon Press, Los Angeles, 1996), *Knuzevna Rec* (Belgrade), *Notus, Ploughshares, Poetry USA, Ribot, The San Diego Reader, Scarlet, Sulfur, Talus* (London), and *The World*.

The drawing on page 101, by Arie Galles, *Auschwitz-Birkenau, Station #1*, is from the artist's *Fourteen Stations* suite (© 1995 by Arie Galles).

Manufactured in the United States of America
New Directions Books are printed on acid-free paper.
First published as New Directions Paperbook 828 in 1996
Published simultaneously in Canada by Peguin Books Canada Limited

Library of Congress Cataloging-in-Publication Data

Rothenberg, Jerome, 1931–
   Seedings & other poems / Jerome Rothenberg.
      p.   cm.
   ISBN 0–8112–1331–5
   I. Title.
  PS3568.086S38   1996
  811'.54—dc20   96–14180
                                          CIP

New Directions Books are published for James Laughlin
by New Directions Publishing Corporation,
80 Eighth Avenue, New York 10011

For Matthew, Nancy, Sadie

new birth that enters
with the sun
each morning   comes to us

as it has come
for generations   aeons
opening the light

the place of entry
for all who live & die

•

this poem for our son
his wife & daughter
& the millennium to come

7/22/93

CONTENTS

14 STATIONS

SEEDINGS

SEEDINGS

for Robert Duncan

I was given a poem in the dream . . . a poem I read out
loud . . . where I could feel the words coming in bursts
but couldn't salvage them . . . I only knew the poem's
name was "seedings" & that it followed after a performance
of "cokboy" in which I had to improvise the final lines,
unable to remember what they were. . . . Between poems
I made a comment about Duncan's peculiar way of reading,
knowing he was dead but seeing him sitting in the audience
& nodding at me when I started reading.

1

Now in the dream
I read aloud
the poem of seedings,
like the last time I saw you,
& how it opens me
to further words, new
definitions,
as I see you sitting there,
old friend,
alive, to hear my stammer
like your own,
that mark of poetry upon
each poet's tongue,
I call the listeners to hear
in us, while laughing,
crying,
at some other poem I read before,
obsessive words
we all can nod our heads to,
but I could not find
the ending,
not for all the years of reading it
aloud, & heard somebody say

—not you but somebody—
time is the thief of language
(meaning tongues)
like that the cat gets hold of

2

shadow of George Oppen,
having lost
his words, the shadow of a poet
he'd become,
or Blackburn speaking of it
first: I've lost
my verbs & nouns,
my alphabets
& birthdays,
who am no kind of man without
those seedings,
sparks,
the pain obliterating all
or else the mind
retreating from itself,
like Williams in his old age
—& no flight of small
cheeping birds—
but "No . my hands
are tongue-tied . You have . . . made
a record in my heart
                    Goodbye."
(Blackburn records it)
or my mother or my brother looking
much like you did, Paul,
the mouth become a hole
the language jammed into our cavities
—cancer aphasia alzheimers—
the poets punished for their poetry,
sharing their punishment with other beings
or what happens
simply
when the mind & body—little

sad machine—
starts shutting down

3

the cat is death,
the thief of language,
meaning tongues,
enough to construct a mythos on
at last   old male cat
comes in thru his window
to talk to him
although it finds him voiceless,
waving kindly to my son
who stands outside
—hi, Paul—
the tape is turning, sends
my own voice back to me
he must have placed with care
there on the reel
to mark our visit—
& this was twenty years ago
& more now   a time no cat
could possibly survive
during which time the deaths have come
increasingly,
reality by that thrown back
into the cat's mind,
where all reality resides
till death disrupts it
& erases world & time at once
your time & mine, Paul,
as it erases words,
stares out at you
so big   it trembles
on your screen,
ascends your vertebrae,
gone into dust by now,
poor spook,
our voices on the tape

already gone for you
although you labored to engrave it,
lugging that big old box around
—from reel to reel
to still more real—
when there was a world to live in
& the words to know it by
quickly came into mind & hand,
remember?
—no there is no memory
among the dead
& even when you write them down
it isn't I who speak
these words but you
& only for a time

4

Write a poem for the dead & leave a place for all the dead
to enter. . . . Consider their words as seeds or treat the
dead themselves as seeds . . . & see a cat's face as the face
of death. . . . Go into the cat's mind . . . an apotheosis
of Cat. . . . Directive: since the cat is living there, attend
to how it stalks, the way it moves through space & time.

but death abolishes
all space & time—
like Gertrude's Oakland,
like the cat's mind,
where no there is
& the world appears as constant pulses,
present running into present
only void of past
& future
so the cat becomes a number
lying on its side,
the cat becomes a distant echo,
one who vanishes
without a word,

the ocean convulsing to the sound of cat,
the way the world convulsed
& dreamt itself,
the dream became our lives,
by which we marked the world's
beginnings & will mark
its end   so simple
that there is no world to prove
beyond us   as the cat's world
ends when cat goes
into death, takes with it
what must be memory of garden,
crooked stems & whiteveined lilies
on black stalks,
& does the poem exist
when there is no one there
to hear it,
when the poet's throat is emptied
of his verbs & nouns,
lost brother walking on
some lonely ridge
discharging
holy tears,
too far into his death
to call it back
the birds around him in the thousands,
the gulls above the bridge
so many cries   such fast desires,
cold birds outside his window
his own skin at the world's edge,
crying for his gods
                    / October almost
5 in the afternoon
the words so easily disposed
between myself & you
that I would quote us into life
dear Paul   would trust
the rest to follow
shortly, into life

5

a poem of seedings,
in the traces of

others who have gone before,
from life to life,
those tied to us as friends or kin
we look for in the empty field
& wonder   where
or in what form
they vanished
who were here just yesterday,
still in the mind
we set a place for them,
a house with swollen rooms
& in each room
a solitary dreamer
sits there   face obscured
by sunlight
Is this your mother?
someone asks
or she who took her own life
twice   the first dose
not enough
so that she woke up laughing
in her bitterness   or she
whose father drove her
to her death,
the poet who survived her
shaken, broken
& the other poet's wife,
also so young,
whose photographs surround the room
where I once stayed,
still stay in memory   but
feel it
disappearing too
or dwindling
cut & broken in

reverse
aphasia
until we can make a covenant
with death   we let it
follow us
the walls come tumbling down,
leaving no margin for
our distant lives

6 / DEATH THOUGHTS

[i]
While Thinking of Those Already Dead

since the world was different when they died,
how would they recognize it now?
it is for this reason that it is better that the dead
stay dead   their confusion would only alarm us
who remain alive & sometimes have to think
about the dead & what to say to them
to set things straight

[ii]
Eternal Question

I wonder sometimes what the last word will be
spoken or heard before I die,
& I feel a great sadness not to know it
in advance, or ever know it

[iii]
Illusion

if there is nothing after death,
then there was nothing before death,
& life is the greatest illusion after all,
the way you fell for it
& I did,
there will be nothing behind us when we die

o these are wounds of love
these precious eyes

those who have lived a life of poetry
will die
        & meet the poets
it will be five o'clock
the blanket on the bed will fall away
the fat man will absorb the shock
love brings him   & now
unlike the others in the tunnel
he will forget to crouch
forget the dead who stand before him
blow their words like knives
over his head   beware   beware
the car door opens & a relentless squad
enters the imagination
in which   as in a sylvan clearing
poets mill around a thorn bush
for those who lived a life of poetry
to stare upon   to take the hands of
in their own & touch with lips
so dark the sun can barely reach them
old friends gone beforehand
let me call them one last time
by name   by seeding them
into the poem its body dark with soil
among whom a new fellow comes
the lately fallen ghost
who took her own life   fell
until no sky remained between
the soil & her
depression of the spirit raging
like the hungry ghost
inside her   throws her down
bones throbbing
makes her to feel her tongue
jammed down her throat

hermaphroditic in the shadow of
the phallic altar
there is god (she says) & man
& there are monsters
leading the way to death   among the friends
who wait her presence
those who have lived a life of poetry
whom we will only see once
in that final moment when we join them
before the chill sets in
the bliss of language lost to us
forever   drifting
like mindless phantoms
empty voices
without our verbs & nouns

IMPROVISATIONS

IMPROVISATION NO. 1
Untitled

Moment of stillness under stars when

the doll calls
calendars drop down   her eyes

drop down
(notice them dropping down)

focused on a distant boat   Throbbing
shadow in relief

The boundaries set to break apart

We watch as it unfolds for us
The more we look

the more we can't look   Fading lines

in her imagination

An open cut
water between her legs   Scissors

& lights

The feather merchant's victim
(innocent girl astride his thighs

innocent thrusts no one can stop) Ikon

of Pleasure
Kafka's incredible machine

journeys to magic isles   felt as

nostalgia
The captain crammed in the prow of the old barge

Dreaming the barge

Walking backwards on the pink plank
cryptical messenger

measurable deflections in the magnetic field

IMPROVISATION NO. 2
Spring. The Mother

Where he steps inside, a leaf unmasks itself, to let the face come through, bright in the dark & smiling, opening defracted mirrors, hoses strewn along the carpet.

It is home, a house it is, I walk through to be in it.

Once in spring. No finer love is this than what the hope of love brings through to you.

Unveil.

Drop down there where the sea rises above your waist.

She is a little doll.

We covet where she tries to find the opening & back away from her.

We run into the stars, we hide, we bathe between old bathers.

Who is this who walks here?

First a question.

Second the roll & loll of it, a halfheard prayer.

The first of May is like the early half of dreaming: it is cut in two between two monkeys. There is a gentleman there too. He has a different name, but we remember who he is & where his fingers touch on us.

Come again. Too soon. Too dearly held. A chicken in the arms of someone tall. A mother in the room a mother walks in. Where she turns about. Where she is there for pleasure & the tender promise company can keep when someone asks.

IMPROVISATION NO. 3
Bleached Landscape

The birds circle a tree in never increasing numbers.

.

Beside the sea with traces of vanilla, see how the torn earth sparkles, wrenched from us.

.

The runners barricade themselves against the moon.

.

Clop-clop-clop. You make a sound & pull back with the others. They are called the handsome dreamers.

.

Look, the girl in white cries out, the sun has grown a moustache.

.

We cannot attend to those who die. Take chances shortly but return at noon.

.

The general is talking Turkish. See how small his hands are, only half a man's.

.

Assembled. Marching through the town with flags & sparklers.

.

They who throw a coin into the sea will reap red harvests.

.

Paradise is half a field away.

.

A city jammed onto a landscape like a giant eye.

.

At last their work has been accomplished!
At last the numbers match!

IMPROVISATION NO. 4
Reservoir & Rapture

The perpetual movement of our walking by a reservoir still moves me. It was this kind of place that brought the rapture, that shook down a star. I let a walnut crash against a radiator: thump, it shatters, & the wind runs up a knickered leg. How young the day is, younger than the boys & ponds, stone tables shattering their pingpong fingers, iron trees the muscled ball sails over.

Pandemonium. The first word that we loved was graceless, smelled of other, lesser words. There was a magic that our fathers made for us in sleep: a language rhyming clocks with death. The second was peculiar. Eyes & thighs.

My dear you are a witness. Near & far the pendulum was such a fiction, was the image I drew best on saturdays, saw on the screen & in your sleep.

It shattered like the ice, the rime on windows. In the night it turned into an angel's bird face, when I dreamed of angels. When we woke up powder rattled in our ears & left us waiting with a mouth whose stains were legion. I became my thought.

Distrustful, penitent. An old religious man comes walking by. His neck is buried in a candy-colored scarf that strangles him, that makes his voice so distant birds wouldn't contain it. Paint him with a fish. A mitten wrapped around my hand is like a prayer. Your rhythm half unwinds it. Look & listen. See the glass stuck in its wooly side, the way the fingers curl around the animal. I love the sound of tiny sparks.

You moron! says the friend. He cites the call to battle. There are armies on the cards as there are tigers in the starry heavens. It was the reason why we searched for Blake & found him—stuck a knife into a pillow, watered fields.

I know the seeds of war. They come into the middle of the garden every night & need your helping hand. Step forward! Die so paradise may live. Pale soldiers. Little crystal bears. The further into life we move, the more they die.

IMPROVISATION NO. 5
Gauguin's Freeways

1

The comb its own exhaustion makes, but there are others.
Verticals & simple downers, cruisers on the eagle path, a
way between two stars. It is the sun in mercury, the road
among alliances, the inner dome. I worship calves & clavi-
cles, recall the thin hands of a priest who is a majordomo, a
professor bound to cottages, a comma above tiles.

.

Impressed, embarking. Figures on the boat are numbered,
but the spark escapes the double line & falls, reverberates,
becomes a string of frozen fires.

.

In a house above the sea we stare at kites. The tigers loop,
the eye stays solid in the dancer's head. He pays for cush-
ions, rests his head athwart the patron's legs, becalmed &
innocent inside his vest. Procession is the way to go. The
pace is breathless, always derailing over tar.

2

The date assumes its page, its code assembled by a hand so
hot the lead turns into vapors, do we see it drift away? we
do & try to muzzle it before the sea shuts down. The stores
at Venice. Skateboards turning bodies into smiles.

.

Class acts. An orange is no stranger to the taste between his
lips. A young girl not a circus client but a dreamer. Re-
morse is retrospective. Where the stricken bride speaks
Spanish, there the gulf assumes its further shape, its dis-

tance cleared into a smell, a jar with rubber eyelets, the
prance & dance across its freeways, silver sounds.

3

In night's bordello,
the crush of cardboard boxes,
of crosses,
aspirins.

Old voices once adrift, now dying.

There is a woman, trembles
like a dog.
Pink bodies in the field of Mars.
A rush of semen.

The water that unlocks her silvered hands.

(To occlude is human,
to withdraw divine.)

4

A Conversation Between Monks

—The heartland.
—Harder than the heart.
—A broken treaty.
—Torched.
—Proceed to the next exit.
—Ten.

.

Religious Maxim

What trees the skunk untrains the broken heart.

.

Flame.
Flamingo.
Gone in flames.
Gone fishing.

.

She the mellower,
in mauve,
inspirited by asters,
froth of autumn,
deer tracks.
Crosses by the barn door.
—Beg your pardon.
—Thirty strokes & more.

.

Tacit, Paul Gauguin.
(Pronounce it, as in Latin.)

IMPROVISATION NO. 6
First Song

Man doubles man,
is man man.
Strikes & opens.
Sings.

Is half a bullet.
Glass.
Is man the conqueror,
who wanders forth.

How gaffless.
Gone & gone.
Peculiar.
Glazes eye to eye.

A tray.
A tree.
A three in speaking.
Three by three.

IMPROVISATION NO. 7
American Weather
July 4, 1990

how strange to be in it,
to be in it

fading away again
to zero

as the crowd begins
the slow ride

over fields, the gay
descent

to town   these little men
pretending

on a bright july
a world of flags

unfurling, rising
striped & naked

habitat

obstruction

counterpoints

a field

a resolution

bonny
stripes & stars

IMPROVISATION NO. 8
The Space Allotted

Say it in words.
Hallucination.
Tremble.
Say that umbrellas hide the moon from sight, I cannot
imagine where the bricks will go or who beside the two of us
will haunt this garden.
And so they say it.
So they say & back away from saying.
A cautious bell.
I find the nerve is ice in my machine, it sparks & lights
a new enclosure.
There is so much gas for working here & little time.
The rhyming goes where rhyming was first gone.
Which ends it.
But not quite. Not half a league away from day.
A space ship cruises past a second space ship in the
space allotted.
Awkward in her uniform she plots the stars.
Vestigial, barely famous, do I send another line?
A fax will carry it, a bird will bear it to the distant shore.
In Iceland rocks are blue & shiny—like the earth.

IMPROVISATION NO. 9
Mochē

The hand opens. Darkness.
The fingers spread apart. A fish.
The eight & eighty, sometimes told, refresh us.
In the lesser twilight someone walks inside his darkness
to be swallowed whole.
A peanut is a sacred mystery for those before us,
for the man inside the web, a source of light.
How brilliant, Moon says to her stars.
Proceed by walking to the sky's edge.
We will find you there,
the water is our guide.
A life lived with no sister is an unlived life.
It is dark again & we are bought & sold.
Surrender, says the dream,
& dreams us,
until it comes back to us,
awake.

IMPROVISATION NO. 10
Forgetting

This body her body shining moving backwards in the night
that grows gathers around us

The blackfaced clowns the rows of grieving marchers hold-
ing torches flashlights in the growing dark

I love you sings a child but he is lost as you are as you were
always lost & I was lost beside you

What is life if it goes on without us

What is the world if it can slough us off if daily it will slough
off millions

The living have outpaced the dead I cry for them I watch
them vanishing in *time*

Remove an eye there is no darkness underneath but there
is always darkness

Pry out a tongue there is no speech left in the throat no
shape of words emerging through the gullet

In my lungs a universe is brought to heel

Duodenum is winter's cave

The sex of man is tethered by a single thread it won't escape
the earth will fall from you & shape the fatal balance

Your legs will bring you to the void of ghosts

A gulf here & a sharp hypotenuse the others two by two will
race into your mind

Tomorrow

See the plane take off while we stand underneath & watch
we search the sky this one time when we know we can't
return to earth

I write this in a dream a passage between worlds my every-
thing my single star & guide

Now is the time to make your peace with earth

Now is the time to overcome forgetting

Twentieth Century Unlimited

TWENTIETH CENTURY UNLIMITED

as the twentieth century winds down
the nineteenth begins
again
      it is as if nothing happened
though those who lived it thought
that everything was happening
enough to name a world for & a time
to hold it in your hand
unlimited   the last delusion
like the perfect mask of death

ANGER: A DREAM

The jaw drops down & is
lamentable,
so much now that it hurts
to speak about

& more than pain
the sparks fly like a vision
to the eye, the eye
that now breaks open

leaves a residue behind,
a viscous matter,
little lies
we cannot tame

but helps us let them out
beyond the hurt,
the dream we dream about
that we are in a dream

that someone strikes at us
for lying, that the jaw
drops down & off,
the eye reclaims its night

in wetness
like a
perfect residence
for pain

PAIN

as a name to call the poem by

this is the fact of life   this rises
every time we move
this is the burden of the killers

see how they walk around
they find a pleasure in it

because what nature gives
isn't enough
the task of life is its enlargement

enlightenment is also pain

as love is

THE ROAD TO HOLLAND
9/30/93

ghosts of ardennes
rise from the mist
& fill the highway

where your foot is slippery
against the gas—
riding to Liège

.

cows at their business
bow a hundred heads

.

a town named for the church
—l'église—
reads "legalise"

.

the man in the orange suit
along the road
is bald & fat

a little tuft of white hair
& looking miserable
in this wet air

.

mist turns to fog—
road turns to Liège

.

cows turn to crows
with just a single *v*

(the poem becomes
a poem of turnings)

.

every 5 kilometers
another poem

cut trunks of trees
along the roadside

.

over the air,
a military air

& on the ground,
uprooted trees:

a hillside bare
of trees

.

—what color
  is that tree?

—the season's
  color

.

"good morning,
ladies all"

the English voices sing

recordings from old
gramophones

millennia ago

.

near Tilff we find
old sun emerging

colors stirring
in the trees

.

Dark
Brick
Belgium

.

a town called Stein
a saint called Geertruid

.

Holland in the sun
along the Maas

(called SUNNY HOLLAND)

ALTAR PIECES / 1993

1

The Tree of Jesse

"people dangling
"in the air

"the patron needs
"a shave

/

David strums a harp
another
blows a conch

/

which jewish kings
are wearing
the striped socks?

2

Saint Agnes

wonders,
as the sheep climbs up
her dress

3

A First Enactment

Four Augustinian canons meditate beside an open grave on
the transitoriness of human life in the presence of Saints
Augustine & Jerome and Mary & Elizabeth, enacting the
Visitation.

4

Saint Lucy

stands in flames

a bearded man
is fanning
with a bellows

while a soldier
drives a sword
into her neck

& on the steps above
a man & woman sit
his hand atop her breast

5

The Adoration

a magus sniffs
a baby's arm

6

This Mary Magdalene

has hebrew on
her bodice

& a naughty smile

Amsterdam 1993

AT THE DAHLEM

Standing Coyote

stands.

Old Fire God

cries out.

.

A Chief

drinks water
from a bowl

as I drink
coffee

(hanging from his sides:
two heads)

.

A Woman

with long breasts
& swollen feet.

.

The Man

with shells around
his waist

holds hands
together

ready to dive in.

.

A Jaguar

in a turtle's shell.

.

A Man's Head

grows between
his legs.

.

Half Man

Half lobster.

Half Skeleton

Half conch.

.

A "Happy" Man

A bell around
his neck

he holds his small arms
opened wide

& smiles.

.

A Man in Anguish

throws his head back

holds his belly

runs

.

The Prisoners

run naked

birds & cactuses
on every side.

.

Pins

thru her nose
her breasts
her knees

her toes
her pelvis.

Scissors
in each hand.

.

Cat Face / Seated

Open mouth:
4 teeth above
2 teeth below.

Tongue hanging out.

3 bells around
his neck.

Great padded
hands & feet

with claws.

.

Another Cat / Our Father

His tail ends
in an arrow.

He shows
a yard-long
tongue.

.

Sri Lanka God

His eyes pop
from his head.

And in his hand
he holds
two naked bodies.

Another
in his mouth.

He stands atop
a smiling mask.

Four cobras
flank him

& a battery of
smiling masks.

He wears a crown
of cobras.

.

The Two White Dolls

have bloodred
hands.

Berlin
November 1993

PICTURES OF THE CRUCIFIXION

Mary of Prague

in wood,
holds up the stricken
Christ.

Mary of Prague

in paint,
up tight against
his side.

2

At Golgotha

One angel watches the blood spurt in his cup.

A second swings a censer in the air while flying.

The third one buzzes around his feet to catch the drip-
pings.

3

The Suffering of the Thieves

A devil steals
the thief's soul

—or an angel—

& the soul's
a tiny babe.

4

The Death of Mary

Christ holds her
in his lap

as child.

5

Jesus

with medusa hair—
all snakes

Prague 1993

ALTAR PIECES / 1994

Harrowing Hell

Hell as
an octopus,
or jelly fish

another devil
at the side
with bat wings

& a lion rump.

.

Blood

dripping down
his side

a pool of blood
lodged in his groin

threads down
his leg.

.

Saint Denis (i)

sees his head
struck off

his headless body
at their feet.

.

Saint Denis (ii)

holds his head
between his hands

his little terrier
still at his feet

(throw him a bone!)

.

Babe on Lap
holds apple

another babe
reads book.

.

The Dead Man

standing in his coffin
blows
a white bird from his mouth

an old man
at the window
blows it back.

.

Three Prophets
like three rogues

a hand behind
the beardless one

holds up a sign.

.

The Saint's Cup

filled with snakes.

.

A Dead Hand
from behind a beam

the coffin tilted
on a rock

a bird, no bigger
than a mouse

moves down the floor.

.

Mother & Child
in ruined castle

flying babes
on every side.

.

The One-Eyed Flutist

hooks you with
his good brown eye.

.

"Eva Prima Pandora"

is the new Pandora
dressed as nymph.

50

The Magdalene

with glove on,
holds her breast

with ungloved hand,
his calf.

.

The Funeral of Love

is followed by
a gang of poets.

Paris
November 1994

A PARADISE OF POETS

1

He takes a book down from his shelf & scribbles across a page of text: *I am the final one*. This means the world will end when he does.

2

In the Inferno, Dante conceives a Paradise of Poets & calls it Limbo.

Foolishly he thinks his place is elsewhere.

3

Now the time has come to write a poem about a Paradise of Poets.

A MESSAGE FOR THE ONE
WHO WALKS HERE, YES

she is too busy walking with her hands full
yes she turns away

    I suffer as you do too
    as we have always suffered
    not from insolence
    & not from too much perspiration
    but from the desire to be taller than this room
    & to include it   yes there is a message
    for the one who walks here, yes

we want to give it to her here & now
to put it in its place
What would it be like
(he thought) a room in which the furniture
is made of ice   only the ice is rock
it doesn't melt
there are no puddles, cold & black,
from melting ice

    Into which room a woman walks
    whose hands are taken up with shining objects:
    glasses, thimbles, lakes that catch the sun, a misty eye
    bright baubles, things to open other things
    "my life" the man thinks "would be lost without
    such women"

And as he falls asleep the door
comes off its hinges
"leave the man alone" (it cries)
"& find a place to spend the night
yourself"   a message for the one who walks here
in her sleep

Across the alley: birds
a factory   how small a factory can be
for those who work in it
how large for those who walk away
they find themselves alive & crying
under the sun

A blue sun (says the man) will never melt the ice
a bird will fly into the mirror
"say goodbye to us & leave us helpless"
but the woman won't obey him
yes here where she leaves her name,
even to write it backwards
"ice is the substance of our life on earth
the bed on which we lie"

A LAW OF BODIES

ice against your hand,
the palm upraised,
feels hot

& leaves no moment,
not a point in time,
for reminiscence

when I hold your hand
in mine   it is the shadow
not the light

that burns

TWO UNTITLED POEMS

[I]

WHEN I SIT WITH YOU
across the table
Lorca's eyes rise up
between us

& they stare
they are
two flageolets
2 castanets

cassettes of little
pleasures   set
into a glass wall
broken into pieces

otherwise   how stare
how spare a glance
for where a star swims by
how glare at Lorca

glaring past you
like a glass
on fire   a shadow's
brilliance

still open to the sun

[II]

IN MYSTIC SIGHT, IN MYSTIC NUMBERS
arising from the dirt pile
he looks up & sees the world look up

around him
         & then he sees
the world look down, prehensile,
wrapped into a single body,

brown, as big as anything,
so that exclusion must remain a minus,
a thing that can't be counted although he looks around,

he looks back & tries to count it:
magic is its name, black thoughts
its means of living in his mind

& being counted   all day long
pursued by someone who pursues it,
he is like a fallen soul who finds

a crust of bread, unnamed,
the little savage,
scrambling up a foreign street

& jams it, helpless,
drowning, down a hungry sister's
mouth & throat

ROC AMADOUR
Black Virgin

black virgin,
sparkling crown
& sparkling
necklace

child sits on her lap
but distant
african in darkness,
against a wall of light

green stones inserted
in the altar,
boats in the arches
swinging

bell in ceiling
ringing for
lost sailors

in the large hall
Jesus
hanging from a tree
like Judas,
suicided man

a heavy body,
dark nails
through his hands,
blood dripping
down his chest

the skeletons of dead men
dancing on the outer wall

THE WOULD-BE SUICIDE INSIDE HIS CELL
A Kafka Variation

a fire at the core lights up
my nakedness   my shoes
begin to burn
the prisonyard ignites & shows
a gallows
from which a holy being dangles
his own core covered by a special garment,
what a holy being
what a residue of holiness around his core
like everything that's holy
like a prisoner
a would-be suicide inside his cell
his shoes stripped from him   opening
his nakedness & mine
the residue igniting in the fire

DESPAIR & DISASTER—2 MULTIPLYING FORCES—HE HELD ONTO AS HIS LIFE RAN QUICKLY OUT

1   An interchange of flutes.

2   quickly / swiftly

3   The man starts to walk
    up the mountain.
    The woman joins him halfway
    up the slope.
    They glide along—like
    flying.

4   Upside down.
    Then downside up.

5   THE BIRDS—PRECISELY BIRDS—
    they are formationless
    with nobody to tell the limits,
    therefore untold, burnt
    each finds a corner of the house to buzz,
    to slam against,
    the curtain fast descends
    this ends
            bird presences.

LORCA VARIATION 34
A Book of Hours

3:00 P.M.

The green man, more a man
than most, took a scissors,
cut the sky with it,
let a river loose
till it became
a sea, the way that yellow
turns to gold,
his scissors tore its blue
apart, his lips
grown pale with dust,
the branches broke
& from the west a man rode up,
who saw the west in ruins,
Pan sat with a zither
heaping sadness upon sadness
earth upon air
until the sun itself was lost,
the air as murky
as the soul of man
he bathes in it
he sits inside
a molten pool
a catherine wheel spins overhead
a hundred pinwheels

6:00 P.M.

They set the snake loose
where the weathercocks
were twisting   slowly
day was settling on the fountain
sunset dropping from
their beaks   we drove our boat

around while evening
let its tail fall
& the half moon hunkered down
would turn forever blue among
its blue birds

7:00 P.M.

Venus waits in front of you
& trembles   will tomorrow
ever come, she thinks
& everything be like it was
inside the well
or will the stars be there
reflected,
shivering
she like a girl will be
the first to raise it

8:00 P.M.

What a sweetheart he has,
who is wrapped in her blindfold,
can't see him,
not for all her one thousand eyes
like a dragon's   or tongues
as loud as the wind's
she will lose him at last
in a crowd
even though she stares down from her sky
a shivering Venus

9:00 P.M.

In sight of the river,
a river that looks like
brushed velvet   an island

shaped like a heart
but bloodless
the breeze that skims over
is soft as a kiss
where a cistern lies open
ready to swallow the sky,
an olive grove vanishes
vanishes   words
cover everything
pass them along to your lady
make sure the color is blue

THE DISPERSAL

1

figures in flight,
how quickly through the forests

run & hide, their game
never over

not until the forests fall,
all forests in the world

all worlds between here
& an empty hole

the dead & living fall through
the messengers & passengers

fingers holding
coins & rings

who drop down headlong
into a world of lights

their cries have shaped with sound
remembered, with a wheel

still spinning   highways
that shine with fat

the father in a field of money
lost among the spirits

who will find them, who finds
their common ground

2

it is the allure of foresters
the allure of give me more,

my hand is reaching toward you
out of its broken cloth, fingers

stained red with blood
too thick to hold the moon up

but lets it be the moon
that slips, crushes against

the pavement   it is run & hide
your face, your absent eyes

fastened on mine

3

the price of bread
is what it takes,

too thick to hold the moon up,
while running beside

the factories, again
around the broken wall,

to find the road
the village where a family

of jews still lives
from there into the mystery

of huts, of caves
foremost, running from their dogs,

his fingers
dropping gold along the way

or pebbles
that the ground sucks up,

the gentile fondles
sadly, lets him foretell

his heartbreak
through a loaded gun

4

the old house spurns him
& the wind does

the people who pursue
old occupations

& who have no time
no sense of how we stand

& fall   our eyes
the windows of our souls

containers of an age
left with the dead

never to be recovered
or expressed

the pain of money, clutched
tight inside his fist

& offered to the nearest
enemy, the furthest

friend

5

Requiem

from there into the mystery
of be at home

be soothed, the past
also will burn away

there is no other explanation
save what death brings

into the mystery of pain
the mystery of cut wrists,

little houses
battered by the wind

they are so in love with sleep
& other mysteries

the mystery of what you are
is what you die for,

(therefore die!)

of when he turns away
you plant a coin on him

then bow & enter
a village near the house of death

still run by jews,
still robbers

pin you against a wall
& take your gold watch

from you   sobbing
in the wind, the smell of apples

in the wind, the mystery
of apples

of the white flesh, at the core
a modest drop of blood

a fire that is fire's
mystery, that holds

so many colors, you could croak
from colors

& you do

& when you do

you die

& enter through the gate
again, the secret gate
the black hole turning white

turns into night

PROLOGOMENA TO A POETICS

for Michael McClure

. . . .

Poet man walks between dreams
He is alive, he is breathing freely
thru a soft tube like a hookah.
Ashes fall around him as he walks
singing above them.
Oh how green
the sun is where it marks
the ocean.
Feathers drift atop the hills
down which the poet man
keeps walking, walking
a step ahead of what he fears,
of what he loves.

. . . .

Why has the poet failed us?
Why have we waited, waited for the word to come again?
Why did we remember what the name means
only to now forget it?
If the poet's name is god how dark the day is
how heavy the burden is he carries with him.
All poets are jews, said Tsvetayeva.
The god of the jews is jewish, said a jew.
It was white around him & his voice
was heavy,
like a poet's voice in winter,
old & heavy,
crackling,
remembering frozen oceans in a summer clime,
how contrary he felt
how harsh the suffering was in him,
let it go!
The poet is dreaming about a poet
& calls out.
Soon he will have forgotten who he is.

. . . .

Speak to the poet's mother,
she is dead now.
So many years ago she left her father's clime.
His *father* too.
The tale of wandering is still untold,
untrue. The tale of who you are,
the tale of where the poem can take us,
of where it stops
& where the voice stops.
The poem is an argument with death.
The poem is priceless.
Those who are brought into the poem can never leave it.
In a silver tux the poet in the poem by Lorca
walks down the hall to greet the poet's bride.
The poet sees her breasts shine in the mirror.
Apples as white as boobs,
says Lorca.
He is fed the milk of paradise,
the dream of every poet man
of every poet bride.
The band plays up
the day unstops & rushes out to greet
another night.

. . . .

Is the black poet
black?
And is the creation of his hands & throat
a black creation?
Yes, says the poet man
who wears three rings,
the poet man who seeks the precious light,
passes the day beside a broken door
no one can enter. Hold it shut,
the god cries & the jew rolls over
in his endless sleep.
Gods like little wheels glide past him
down the mountain road where cats live

in a cemetery guarded by his father's star,
a poet & a bride entangled in the grass,
his hands are black
his eyes the whitest white
& rimmed with scarlet.
Hear the drumbeat,
heart.
The blacks have landed on the western shore
the long lost past of poetry revives.

. . . .

Our fingers fail us.

Then tear them off! the poet cries
not for the first time.
The dead are too often seen filling our streets,
who hasn't seen them?
A tremor across the lower body,
always the image of a horse's head
& sandflies.
A woman's breast & honey.
She in whose mouth the murderers stuffed gravel
who will no longer speak.
The poet is the only witness to that death,
writes every line
as though the only witness.

AN ORACLE FOR DELFI

for Demosthenes Agrafiotis

small men chipping—
writing on the walls

THE STONES OF DELFI (I)

1

the stones speak

2

the stones laugh

3

we—like all poets—
have a taste for stones

STONES & BONES

of giants

1

eat a stone

2

plant stones & watch them grow

3

stone soup

THE STONES OF DELFI (II)

here is an edge to stone,
here is a cry with splinters driven
into the bone   the clavicle

responding in pain
here where the pain is nearly solid
gravitates toward stone itself

the voice in stone is letters
broken marks   the small men chipping
writing on the walls

will build a world in stone
where we can live   & find it
beautiful & lonely

the mark of higher cultures
but once shattered into shapes
becomes so primary

it takes your breath away
—those loplop columns
arising toward the sky at delfi

no civic order merely
architecture   but the promise of
new wildernesses

where the stones speak
the stones laugh
towering above their witnesses

the stones drop to the earth
we sow them into place
& watch them grow

like giants
broken bodies of our pasts
false signatures

inscribed by wars
that never end
that leave a chaos always

a paradise of stones

A BULL'S HEAD

eyes made of crystal
snout of jasper
muzzle of mother-of-pearl

blood spurting
thru its mouth

MINOAN ASSETS

a boar's tooth helmet

domestic snakes

THE FUNERAL

1

the bull stretched
on a table

a musician
with 2 flutes
leading a crowd
of women

& the priestess
pouring blood
into a bowl

2

a woman with a crown
brings blood
in buckets

hands them to another
woman
who empties them

between the double
ax blades

birds are perching on

3

behind them
a musician comes
playing a lute with
7 strings

& 3 men walking in
the opposite
direction, holding pictures of
small animals, a boat

the dead man watching
from his tomb
behind the altar

4

a chariot
drawn by horses

another drawn by griffins

& behind each walk
2 women

YOUNG MAN AT KNOSSOS

his head is ringed with
lilies
& with peacock feathers

& he walks or dances
—walks *and* dances—
stiffly to his right

& with his left hand
leads a beast—
some tethered animal

like horse or sphinx

THE PRICE OF ART

a hornet sucks
a drop of honey
from its comb

AT MYKINES

1

in the royal house
a fire pit & smoke hole
at the center

around which men would sit
the walls renewed with paintings
every year

with goat bells somewhere
in the distance

2

with goat bells somewhere
in the distance

or goblins of these mountains
little people

at this time of year

3

making echoes from its walls
we look for goats

invisible, whose lonely bells
are clanging in the air

4

snowcapped arcadia
beyond   small puffs of smoke
marking the Argive plain

where we were too +

+ I too have been there

MOURNING WOMEN
Mycenean

hands raised to heads—
to show distress

IN KLYTEMNESTRA'S TOMB

like a giant bee hive
or a kiva

IN AGAMEMNON'S TOMB+

a fatal hole
with people

+ tube

LAST RITES

gold scales to weigh
the dead man's soul

gold mask to hide
his face

THE DANCERS

hold each other's
shoulders.

YOUNG SATYR

1

kneeling on a rock,
a lion's skin beneath him,
while silenus feeds him
cakes

2

toy vases, bowls
for babes

A MESSAGE TO THE KING:

HALL FALLEN

PHOEBUS GOD WITHOUT A HOME

PROPHETIC LAURELS LOST

THE WATER'S VOICE FORGOTTEN

WATER LANGUAGE SEEPING OUT

THE FLAME
at Delfi

laurel
& barley flour
burning

THE ATHLETE

having finished wrestling
scrapes the dirt & oil
that cakes his body

while a slave (a young boy)
offers him a bowl
of spicy oils—his dead dog

staring up at him

LOPLOP & THE SIREN
For Max Ernst

bird with a woman's
head, or
woman with a bird's

THE GODDESS (1)

riding on a horse

THE GODDESS (2)

wears a long dress
with an apron

& her breasts are bare

THE GODDESS (3)

a snake around
her body

THE WOMEN (1)

women squeezing nipples

.

a nipple like a star

THE WOMEN (2)

for Man Ray

a woman like a violin

.

with folded arms

THE WOMEN (3)

two breasts in gold:
gold eyes

THE WOMEN (4)

snakes crawling up her arms
they stretch their heads toward her tiara
on which a panther sits

THE WOMEN (5)

women standing with
raised arms—
birds flying from their heads

adorned with pods
of poppies

THE WOMEN (6)

a woman on a swing

.

a sacred tree
with doves

THE WOMEN (7)

dancing legs

A JEWELED NECKLACE
Phaistos

glass paste
gold
carneol
faïence
amethyst
etc.

FROM THE CAVE OF EILETHYIA
Crete

loving couples—

pregnant women—

women suckling babes

THE SEA AT SUNIO
For Marianne Moore

the bluest place
I've never seen

THE SILVER TRADE

1

by workers
strapped into a cage-sized
space

2

poor slaves,
whose children finish up
the job

to bring the silver
to the light

*Cape Sunio, Greece
December 1992*

LAURION

with workers' houses
all around—
the hills torn open,
forming caves
until—in rage—
they tore the boss's statue
from its perch

THE IKON (1)

a bishop with a dog's head
& his rump in front

THE IKON (2)

in worship of an empty cross
a wreath remains on

THE IKON (3)

small head
huge pectorals
arms withered

THE IKON (4)

a pile of wings & feathers
from which an angel's face
peeped out

THE IKON (5)

at the navel of
the world
—the church—

an eagle with a snake
gripped in its claws
becomes
a snake-faced eagle

THE IKON (6)
At Dafni

white bearded devil
surrounded by locks & keys

white bearded adam
arisen from the dead

THE IKON (7)

Pantocrator
with a compass
makes a world

Blake rightly calls
Urizen

JOHN'S APOTHEOSIS
For shamans

wingd angel
bearded
stands above the severed head
he points at

holding a cross & skull
in hand
a tree & ax
beside him

or is it him still
looking down
in pain
at what he was?

HANDS

for Lizzie Calligas

looking at her hand
she saw an eye
& that the eye was crying
water had slid between her fingers
red with rust
& made a pressure she could only ease
by tonguing   licking up
the sweet red juices
& a hand was also in the sky
beside the sun & over it
it flew   spun sideways
upside down
until it brought the night to pass
"I live with hands"
the man thought
sitting in her light
& reached down to his ankles
snapped the lines
that held the other's soul in place
with hands, he thought,
the secret is Elefsis
where the daughter dropt into the earth
oh seed, oh secret eikon
burnt into my hand
like stigma, like stigmata
rays of sunlight
on the flesh
or into it
& the words turn cold & hard like steel
that cuts the page
then rides across our bellies
like a knife
over whatever part of us
the life will flow from   seedings
that reach us from a wasted dream
to make a poem of seedings

like poems & photographs of hands
all of us share   & think
"how classical it is
"how it revolves & leaves us hanging
"this reminiscence of our lives
"alive & dead

SPETSES IN WINTER

1

was more like maine's
dark coast   the way
we walked around it
combing the ground for shards

& in the rain we found
Marina's shrine
(not Mary's, someone said)
in which she stood

triumphant,
sandaled foot on
devil's head,
her face lit

by a crazy smile

2

the wind rose
& the weather—lost to us
in greek—reported
sleet & snow across the isthmus

oh the pleasures of
the single cotton cloth
& inner heat

3

"does an indian eat eggs
"the way a greek does?

14 STATIONS

for Arie Galles

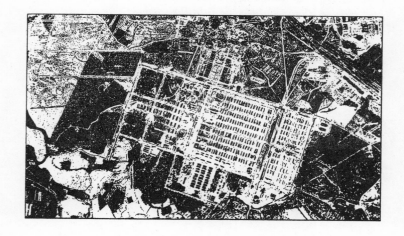

Auschwitz-Birkenau, Station #1 (Arie Galles)

The full series of fourteen poems was written to accompany Arie Galles's monumental charcoal drawings derived from World War II aerial views of the principal Nazi extermination camps— each with an attendant railroad station—known even then to have been the sites of holocaust. As Galles worked from documentary photographs to establish some pretense at distance (= objectivity), I decided to objectify by turning again to gematria *(traditional Hebrew numerology) as a way to determine the words and phrases that would come into the poems. The counts were made off the Hebrew and/or Yiddish spellings of the camp names, then keyed to the numerical values of words and word combinations in the first five books of the Hebrew Bible. It is my hope that this small degree of objective chance will not so much mask feeling or meaning as allow them to emerge.*

THE FIRST STATION: AUSCHWITZ-BIRKENAU

now the serpent:

I will bring back
their taskmasters
crazy & mad

will meet them
deep in the valley
& be subdued

separated in life
uncircumcised, needy
shoes stowed away

how naked they come
my fathers
my fathers

angry & trembling,
the serpents
you have destroyed

their faces remembered
small in your eyes,
shut down, soiled

see a light
take shape in the pit,
someone killed

torn in pieces
a terror, a god,
go down deeper

THE SECOND STATION: BABI YAR

he was angry
& smelled
like the righteous

slew
the clean & pure,
ran over them

& they went down
before us
faint

& streaked,
the bars
along the way

increased & multiplied
before our eyes
their place

spread far & wide,
was like my spirit
& my sword

that made you see

THE THIRD STATION: BUCHENWALD

deliver me
from them

your cattle
rising

your assembly
lords of fat

deliver me
from color

THE FOURTH STATION: BELZEC

of those who had escaped,
the children foremost,
he would take some as witnesses

"leave me to drink
"among the goats
"that you may eat & I be eaten

"when life becomes a terror
"your strength against the children
"& her children blotted out

THE FIFTH STATION: BERGEN-BELSEN

1

gates
round about me

I knew
& you know

& she had compassion
(alive)

a carcass
a carcass

& a dancing
carcass

2

& I will kill
the fat
& the fat ones

the wicked
the he-goats
your mistress

conceived
like a coat
& torn off

like the twenty
those you ran over
& numbered

& like those
I will kill

THE SIXTH STATION: GROSS-ROSEN

& naked there among
the swarming things

we saw them
in the dung

bright spots
bright spots

that she did stare at
& would see them burn

THE SEVENTH STATION: DACHAU

heart
dim
& sore

his hands
slow
& heavy

& so he looked,
his glory
weeping

THE EIGHTH STATION: CHELMNO

1

A Chorus of Children

we dreamed
& he changed:
an armed man
but delicate,
driven,
someone who touches us,
touches
our thighs,
strips us naked,
to wound us,
a fugitive,
evil,
aggrieved,
who punishes,
slays us
at evening

2

A Chorus of Survivors

the word
that you feared
like hail
on the mountain
& feared
what would cause it to shine,
to be seen,
like her belly,
like hooks,
like the wheat
on our altars,
all will be eaten,

will not be
a sacrifice
there with the nations,
but a curse
in her womb

THE NINTH STATION: TREBLINKA

the voices, thunders
& the voices
of our kin
that they will bring in
from the top

the kingdoms gathering
to kill us
& you will wave
o Israel
& will submit yourself

& I will set apart
the sum of them
the thunders, voices
& the thunders
I will watch & will take heed

THE TENTH STATION: MAUTHAUSEN

your camp
brings me
the war
that bore you,

made you inherit
the plague,
your children
torn from you,

your hands that spawned
the offspring of
the nations,
a stone against them

from my hand,
my hand against them
& a plague
between us

THE ELEVENTH STATION: MAIDANEK

1

a thing
spoken
speaks in me

I see
the spoken
thing

a word
hail
pestilence

& from your face
a curse
is poured out

& a bone
is set in motion
spoken

in disgust
to see
the one who speaks it

2

a foreigner,
you say,
the dew like blood

her city
broken
empty for her sake

has blessed you,
seed of them
I will pursue

& you will say
in blood:
leave me alone

THE TWELFTH STATION: SOBIBOR

1

as he had spoken
from the wilderness:
be fruitful!

(& they were fruitful)

so he could blind them
with a fist
& cut them—

& she could take from them
the vision of
his cities

2

a skin
harp
& a boil

according to its words

how blind
& evil
like its skin

your words
erased

THE THIRTEENTH STATION: RAVENSBRUCK

1

in my name she placed
an offering of dust

an offering of graves
where she lay empty

desolate, lay guilty
for her pleasures

in my name, the lamb
approaching

placed the basin
at her neck

throughout your generations

2

For Rachel, twice:

she turned aside,
I thought,
the wood, the thorns
wounding my thighs

& when they came
& carried her away
he gave them numbers
by the sword

a bell
for those with numbers

THE FOURTEENTH STATION: STUTTHOF

the evil water
in my dream

has emptied out
their cities

like my mouth
a hole

& in the blood
they burn

they turn them
into smoke